PEA SOUP

for the PISSED off Soul

This journal belongs to:

Name: _____

Phone: _____

JOURNAL YOUR WAY TO INNER PEAS

By Raquel Murray

A 10th Step Journey to Inner Peas

If you have been around the tables of any 12-step community long enough, you know that there are plenty of common sayings floating around. For example, "One Day at a Time." "To Thine Own Self Be True." "Think, Think, Think." "Easy Does It." And the panacea of all ills; "Write About It."

Though writing is the best solution, it's a solution most of us don't really like.

Why don't we like it? Most of us don't like putting pen to paper because we know the written inventory is designed to help us see our role. And sometimes no matter how much we do write; we can't see our own faulty behaviors. Sometimes we even think we have no part.

I have learned that sometimes finding my part is as easy as looking at my responses to the offenders and offenses. (See page 67 of the Big Book.)

A friend once said, "She is no doubt 9/10ths responsible for the situation, but on careful inspection you will find your part, and you will ask yourself, what am I going to do about the 1/10th I am responsible for?" That made sense to me, and so started my journey cleaning up my side of the street.

I found myself needing a better tool to write about my irritations. I needed something more fun and less daunting than our (beloved, tried and tested) columns. All hail the columns! But I wanted to open them up a little. So, I began creating this journal as a tool for myself. Then it occurred to me that it might be helpful to others.

My hope is that Pea Soup for the Pissed Off Soul becomes a valuable companion on your journey to clean and sober living. This journal teaches you how to do the dreaded yet liberating work of writing it down. It is a welcoming space to air your feelings and thoughts, without judgment, and with a little fun and love.

I've included a suggested template and a sample of how it is used on the next page that might be helpful, followed by a glossary in the back that will prove useful incorporating recovery terminology into your writing. But, as our program wisely advises us, take what you need and leave the rest. Pea Soup for the Pissed Off Soul is for you in your unique recovery process.

The task ahead of you is never as great as the Power behind you. Carry on!

Raquel

Date: 7/12/2013

1) I am pissed off at: My Boss

2) The cause:

They promoted someone else instead of me.

3) What part of self is affected?
(Self-Esteem) (Pride,) (Ambition,) Security, Personal Relations, (Pocket Book)

4) What was my part? My co-worker often uses their time more wisely than me. They are often early and have completed more projects.

5) Where are my mistakes?
(Self-Seeking,) Selfish, Dishonesty, (Fear)

6) Do I see any harm I caused? I was more concerned about personal recognition than acknowledging my teammates hard work. I put myself above my team.

7) Have I ever done the same thing?
(YES) NO
(circle one)

8) Do I owe an amends?
(YES) NO
(circle one)

Write about it.

Last month, a managerial position became available at my work place. I've worked hard to move up, but my co-worker has as well. If I was to be honest, she worked even harder than me. We both applied for the job, but she got it, not me. When my boss told me the news, I was hurt and confused. It took some time to realize my pride, sense of ambition and self-esteem had all been affected. I want to progress in my career, and not getting the gig made me think less of my own abilities. I worried that my co-workers would think less of me as well. It was hard to acknowledge that – while I do work hard – I could have used my time more wisely this year than I did. I didn't get the job because my co-worker was the better canidate. She is often early to work and succeeds at her professional endeavors. I could learn from her promotion. Also, more importantly, she is my friend. I didn't congratulate her when she got the job. I should apologize to her and give her a big, congratulatory hug! I also plan to set up a meeting with my boss. Not getting the job is a chance to renew my goals, and I'd like to talk with my boss about ways I can improve.

Date:

1) I am pissed off at:

2) The cause:

3) What part of self is affected?
   Self-Esteem,   Pride,   Ambition,   Security,
        Personal Relations,   Pocket Book

4) What was my part?

5) Where are my mistakes?
   Self-Seeking,   Selfish,   Dishonesty,   Fear

6) Do I see any harm I caused?

7) Have I ever done the
   same thing?
   YES   NO
   (circle one)

8) Do I owe an amends?
   YES   NO
   (circle one)

Write about it.

Date:

1) I am pissed off at:

2) The cause:

3) What part of self is affected?
   Self-Esteem,   Pride,   Ambition,   Security,
        Personal Relations,   Pocket Book

4) What was my part?

5) Where are my mistakes?
   Self-Seeking,   Selfish,   Dishonesty,   Fear

6) Do I see any harm I caused?

7) Have I ever done the
   same thing?
   YES   NO
   (circle one)

8) Do I owe an amends?
   YES   NO
   (circle one)

Write about it.

Date:

1) I am pissed off at:

2) The cause:

3) What part of self is affected?
   Self-Esteem,   Pride,   Ambition,   Security,
        Personal Relations,   Pocket Book

4) What was my part?

5) Where are my mistakes?
   Self-Seeking,   Selfish,   Dishonesty,   Fear

6) Do I see any harm I caused?

7) Have I ever done the
   same thing?
   YES   NO
        (circle one)

8) Do I owe an amends?
   YES   NO
   (circle one)

Write about it.

Date:

1) I am pissed off at:

2) The cause:

3) What part of self is affected?
Self-Esteem, Pride, Ambition, Security,
Personal Relations, Pocket Book

4) What was my part?

5) Where are my mistakes?
Self-Seeking, Selfish, Dishonesty, Fear

6) Do I see any harm I caused?

7) Have I ever done the same thing?
YES NO
(circle one)

8) Do I owe an amends?
YES NO
(circle one)

Write about it.

Date:

1) I am pissed off at:

2) The cause:

3) What part of self is affected?
Self-Esteem,   Pride,   Ambition,   Security,
Personal Relations,   Pocket Book

4) What was my part?

5) Where are my mistakes?
Self-Seeking,   Selfish,   Dishonesty,   Fear

6) Do I see any harm I caused?

7) Have I ever done the same thing?
YES   NO
(circle one)

8) Do I owe an amends?
YES   NO
(circle one)

Write about it.

Date:

1) I am pissed off at:

2) The cause:

3) What part of self is affected?
Self-Esteem, Pride, Ambition, Security,
Personal Relations, Pocket Book

4) What was my part?

5) Where are my mistakes?
Self-Seeking, Selfish, Dishonesty, Fear

6) Do I see any harm I caused?

7) Have I ever done the same thing?
YES   NO
(circle one)

8) Do I owe an amends?
YES   NO
(circle one)

Write about it.

Date:

1) I am pissed off at:

2) The cause:

3) What part of self is affected?
Self-Esteem, Pride, Ambition, Security,
Personal Relations, Pocket Book

4) What was my part?

5) Where are my mistakes?
Self-Seeking, Selfish, Dishonesty, Fear

6) Do I see any harm I caused?

7) Have I ever done the same thing?
YES   NO
(circle one)

8) Do I owe an amends?
YES   NO
(circle one)

Write about it.

Date:

1) I am pissed off at:

2) The cause:

3) What part of self is affected?
   Self-Esteem,   Pride,   Ambition,   Security,
        Personal Relations,   Pocket Book

4) What was my part?

5) Where are my mistakes?
   Self-Seeking,   Selfish,   Dishonesty,   Fear

6) Do I see any harm I caused?

7) Have I ever done the
   same thing?
   YES   NO
   (circle one)

8) Do I owe an amends?
   YES   NO
   (circle one)

Write about it.

Date:

1) I am pissed off at:

2) The cause:

3) What part of self is affected?
Self-Esteem,   Pride,   Ambition,   Security,
Personal Relations,   Pocket Book

4) What was my part?

5) Where are my mistakes?
Self-Seeking,   Selfish,   Dishonesty,   Fear

6) Do I see any harm I caused?

7) Have I ever done the same thing?
YES   NO
(circle one)

8) Do I owe an amends?
YES   NO
(circle one)

Write about it.

Date:

1) I am pissed off at:

2) The cause:

3) What part of self is affected?
Self-Esteem, Pride, Ambition, Security,
Personal Relations, Pocket Book

4) What was my part?

5) Where are my mistakes?
Self-Seeking, Selfish, Dishonesty, Fear

6) Do I see any harm I caused?

7) Have I ever done the same thing?
YES NO
(circle one)

8) Do I owe an amends?
YES NO
(circle one)

Write about it.

Date:

1) I am pissed off at:

2) The cause:

3) What part of self is affected?
Self-Esteem, Pride, Ambition, Security,
Personal Relations, Pocket Book

4) What was my part?

5) Where are my mistakes?
Self-Seeking, Selfish, Dishonesty, Fear

6) Do I see any harm I caused?

7) Have I ever done the same thing?
YES   NO
(circle one)

8) Do I owe an amends?
YES   NO
(circle one)

Write about it.

Date:

1) I am pissed off at:

2) The cause:

3) What part of self is affected?
   Self-Esteem,   Pride,   Ambition,   Security,
        Personal Relations,   Pocket Book

4) What was my part?

5) Where are my mistakes?
   Self-Seeking,   Selfish,   Dishonesty,   Fear

6) Do I see any harm I caused?

7) Have I ever done the
   same thing?
   YES   NO
   (circle one)

8) Do I owe an amends?
   YES   NO
   (circle one)

Write about it.

Date:

1) I am pissed off at:

2) The cause:

3) What part of self is affected?
Self-Esteem,   Pride,   Ambition,   Security,
Personal Relations,   Pocket Book

4) What was my part?

5) Where are my mistakes?
Self-Seeking,   Selfish,   Dishonesty,   Fear

6) Do I see any harm I caused?

7) Have I ever done the same thing?
YES   NO
(circle one)

8) Do I owe an amends?
YES   NO
(circle one)

Write about it.

Date:

1) I am pissed off at:

2) The cause:

3) What part of self is affected?
Self-Esteem,   Pride,   Ambition,   Security,
Personal Relations,   Pocket Book

4) What was my part?

5) Where are my mistakes?
Self-Seeking,   Selfish,   Dishonesty,   Fear

6) Do I see any harm I caused?

7) Have I ever done the same thing?
YES   NO
(circle one)

8) Do I owe an amends?
YES   NO
(circle one)

Write about it.

Date:

1) I am pissed off at:

2) The cause:

3) What part of self is affected?
Self-Esteem,   Pride,   Ambition,   Security,
Personal Relations,   Pocket Book

4) What was my part?

5) Where are my mistakes?
Self-Seeking,   Selfish,   Dishonesty,   Fear

6) Do I see any harm I caused?

7) Have I ever done the same thing?
YES   NO
(circle one)

8) Do I owe an amends?
YES   NO
(circle one)

Write about it.

Date:

1) I am pissed off at:

2) The cause:

3) What part of self is affected?
   Self-Esteem,   Pride,   Ambition,   Security,
        Personal Relations,   Pocket Book

4) What was my part?

5) Where are my mistakes?
   Self-Seeking,   Selfish,   Dishonesty,   Fear

6) Do I see any harm I caused?

7) Have I ever done the
   same thing?
   YES   NO
   (circle one)

8) Do I owe an amends?
   YES   NO
   (circle one)

Write about it.

Date:

1) I am pissed off at:

2) The cause:

3) What part of self is affected?
   Self-Esteem,   Pride,   Ambition,   Security,
        Personal Relations,   Pocket Book

4) What was my part?

5) Where are my mistakes?
   Self-Seeking,   Selfish,   Dishonesty,   Fear

6) Do I see any harm I caused?

7) Have I ever done the same thing?
   YES   NO
   (circle one)

8) Do I owe an amends?
   YES   NO
   (circle one)

Write about it.

Date:

1) I am pissed off at:

2) The cause:

3) What part of self is affected?
Self-Esteem, Pride, Ambition, Security,
Personal Relations, Pocket Book

4) What was my part?

5) Where are my mistakes?
Self-Seeking, Selfish, Dishonesty, Fear

6) Do I see any harm I caused?

7) Have I ever done the same thing?
YES   NO
(circle one)

8) Do I owe an amends?
YES   NO
(circle one)

Write about it.

Date:

1) I am pissed off at:

2) The cause:

3) What part of self is affected?
   Self-Esteem, Pride, Ambition, Security,
   Personal Relations, Pocket Book

4) What was my part?

5) Where are my mistakes?
   Self-Seeking, Selfish, Dishonesty, Fear

6) Do I see any harm I caused?

7) Have I ever done the
   same thing?
   YES   NO
   (circle one)

8) Do I owe an amends?
   YES   NO
   (circle one)

Write about it.

Date:

1) I am pissed off at:

2) The cause:

3) What part of self is affected?
   Self-Esteem,   Pride,   Ambition,   Security,
           Personal Relations,   Pocket Book

4) What was my part?

5) Where are my mistakes?
   Self-Seeking,   Selfish,   Dishonesty,   Fear

6) Do I see any harm I caused?

7) Have I ever done the
   same thing?
   YES   NO
   (circle one)

8) Do I owe an amends?
   YES   NO
   (circle one)

Write about it.

Date:

1) I am pissed off at:

2) The cause:

3) What part of self is affected?
   Self-Esteem,   Pride,   Ambition,   Security,
         Personal Relations,   Pocket Book

4) What was my part?

5) Where are my mistakes?
   Self-Seeking,   Selfish,   Dishonesty,   Fear

6) Do I see any harm I caused?

7) Have I ever done the
   same thing?
   YES   NO
   (circle one)

8) Do I owe an amends?
   YES   NO
   (circle one)

Write about it.

Date:

1) I am pissed off at:

2) The cause:

3) What part of self is affected?
Self-Esteem, Pride, Ambition, Security,
Personal Relations, Pocket Book

4) What was my part?

5) Where are my mistakes?
Self-Seeking, Selfish, Dishonesty, Fear

6) Do I see any harm I caused?

7) Have I ever done the same thing?
YES   NO
(circle one)

8) Do I owe an amends?
YES   NO
(circle one)

Write about it.

Date:

1) I am pissed off at:

2) The cause:

3) What part of self is affected?
   Self-Esteem, Pride, Ambition, Security,
   Personal Relations, Pocket Book

4) What was my part?

5) Where are my mistakes?
   Self-Seeking, Selfish, Dishonesty, Fear

6) Do I see any harm I caused?

7) Have I ever done the
   same thing?
   YES   NO
   (circle one)

8) Do I owe an amends?
   YES   NO
   (circle one)

Write about it.

Date:

1) I am pissed off at:

2) The cause:

3) What part of self is affected?
   Self-Esteem, Pride, Ambition, Security,
      Personal Relations,   Pocket Book

4) What was my part?

5) Where are my mistakes?
   Self-Seeking, Selfish, Dishonesty, Fear

6) Do I see any harm I caused?

7) Have I ever done the same thing?
YES   NO
(circle one)

8) Do I owe an amends?
YES   NO
(circle one)

Write about it.

Date:

1) I am pissed off at:

2) The cause:

3) What part of self is affected?
Self-Esteem, Pride, Ambition, Security,
Personal Relations, Pocket Book

4) What was my part?

5) Where are my mistakes?
Self-Seeking, Selfish, Dishonesty, Fear

6) Do I see any harm I caused?

7) Have I ever done the same thing?
YES   NO
(circle one)

8) Do I owe an amends?
YES   NO
(circle one)

Write about it.

Date:

1) I am pissed off at:

2) The cause:

3) What part of self is affected?
   Self-Esteem,   Pride,   Ambition,   Security,
            Personal Relations,   Pocket Book

4) What was my part?

5) Where are my mistakes?
   Self-Seeking,   Selfish,   Dishonesty,   Fear

6) Do I see any harm I caused?

7) Have I ever done the
   same thing?
   YES   NO
   (circle one)

8) Do I owe an amends?
   YES   NO
   (circle one)

Write about it.

Date:

1) I am pissed off at:

2) The cause:

3) What part of self is affected?
Self-Esteem, Pride, Ambition, Security,
Personal Relations, Pocket Book

4) What was my part?

5) Where are my mistakes?
Self-Seeking, Selfish, Dishonesty, Fear

6) Do I see any harm I caused?

7) Have I ever done the same thing?
YES   NO
(circle one)

8) Do I owe an amends?
YES   NO
(circle one)

Write about it.

Date:

1) I am pissed off at:

2) The cause:

3) What part of self is affected?
   Self-Esteem, Pride, Ambition, Security,
   Personal Relations, Pocket Book

4) What was my part?

5) Where are my mistakes?
   Self-Seeking, Selfish, Dishonesty, Fear

6) Do I see any harm I caused?

7) Have I ever done the same thing?
   YES NO
   (circle one)

8) Do I owe an amends?
   YES NO
   (circle one)

Write about it.

Date:

1) I am pissed off at:

2) The cause:

3) What part of self is affected?
Self-Esteem, Pride, Ambition, Security,
Personal Relations, Pocket Book

4) What was my part?

5) Where are my mistakes?
Self-Seeking, Selfish, Dishonesty, Fear

6) Do I see any harm I caused?

7) Have I ever done the same thing?
YES   NO
(circle one)

8) Do I owe an amends?
YES   NO
(circle one)

Write about it.

Date:

1) I am pissed off at:

2) The cause:

3) What part of self is affected?
Self-Esteem,   Pride,   Ambition,   Security,
Personal Relations,   Pocket Book

4) What was my part?

5) Where are my mistakes?
Self-Seeking,   Selfish,   Dishonesty,   Fear

6) Do I see any harm I caused?

7) Have I ever done the
same thing?
YES   NO
(circle one)

8) Do I owe an amends?
YES   NO
(circle one)

Write about it.

Date:

1) I am pissed off at:

2) The cause:

3) What part of self is affected?
Self-Esteem, Pride, Ambition, Security,
Personal Relations, Pocket Book

4) What was my part?

5) Where are my mistakes?
Self-Seeking, Selfish, Dishonesty, Fear

6) Do I see any harm I caused?

7) Have I ever done the same thing?
YES   NO
(circle one)

8) Do I owe an amends?
YES   NO
(circle one)

Write about it.

Date:

1) I am pissed off at:

2) The cause:

3) What part of self is affected?
Self-Esteem, Pride, Ambition, Security,
Personal Relations, Pocket Book

4) What was my part?

5) Where are my mistakes?
Self-Seeking, Selfish, Dishonesty, Fear

6) Do I see any harm I caused?

7) Have I ever done the same thing?
YES   NO
(circle one)

8) Do I owe an amends?
YES   NO
(circle one)

Write about it.

Date:

1) I am pissed off at:

2) The cause:

3) What part of self is affected?
Self-Esteem, Pride, Ambition, Security,
Personal Relations, Pocket Book

4) What was my part?

5) Where are my mistakes?
Self-Seeking, Selfish, Dishonesty, Fear

6) Do I see any harm I caused?

7) Have I ever done the
same thing?
YES   NO
(circle one)

8) Do I owe an amends?
YES   NO
(circle one)

Write about it.

Date:

1) I am pissed off at:

2) The cause:

3) What part of self is affected?
Self-Esteem, Pride, Ambition, Security,
Personal Relations, Pocket Book

4) What was my part?

5) Where are my mistakes?
Self-Seeking, Selfish, Dishonesty, Fear

6) Do I see any harm I caused?

7) Have I ever done the
same thing?
YES   NO
(circle one)

8) Do I owe an amends?
YES   NO
(circle one)

Write about it.

Date:

1) I am pissed off at:

2) The cause:

3) What part of self is affected?
Self-Esteem, Pride, Ambition, Security,
Personal Relations, Pocket Book

4) What was my part?

5) Where are my mistakes?
Self-Seeking, Selfish, Dishonesty, Fear

6) Do I see any harm I caused?

7) Have I ever done the same thing?
YES   NO
(circle one)

8) Do I owe an amends?
YES   NO
(circle one)

Write about it.

Date:

1) I am pissed off at:

2) The cause:

3) What part of self is affected?
Self-Esteem, Pride, Ambition, Security,
Personal Relations, Pocket Book

4) What was my part?

5) Where are my mistakes?
Self-Seeking, Selfish, Dishonesty, Fear

6) Do I see any harm I caused?

7) Have I ever done the same thing?
YES   NO
(circle one)

8) Do I owe an amends?
YES   NO
(circle one)

Write about it.

Date:

1) I am pissed off at:

2) The cause:

3) What part of self is affected?
Self-Esteem, Pride, Ambition, Security, Personal Relations, Pocket Book

4) What was my part?

5) Where are my mistakes?
Self-Seeking, Selfish, Dishonesty, Fear

6) Do I see any harm I caused?

7) Have I ever done the same thing?
YES   NO
(circle one)

8) Do I owe an amends?
YES   NO
(circle one)

Write about it.

Date:

1) I am pissed off at:

2) The cause:

3) What part of self is affected?
Self-Esteem, Pride, Ambition, Security,
Personal Relations, Pocket Book

4) What was my part?

5) Where are my mistakes?
Self-Seeking, Selfish, Dishonesty, Fear

6) Do I see any harm I caused?

7) Have I ever done the same thing?
YES   NO
(circle one)

8) Do I owe an amends?
YES   NO
(circle one)

Write about it.

Date:

1) I am pissed off at:

2) The cause:

3) What part of self is affected?
Self-Esteem, Pride, Ambition, Security,
Personal Relations, Pocket Book

4) What was my part?

5) Where are my mistakes?
Self-Seeking, Selfish, Dishonesty, Fear

6) Do I see any harm I caused?

7) Have I ever done the same thing?
YES   NO
(circle one)

8) Do I owe an amends?
YES   NO
(circle one)

Write about it.

Date:

1) I am pissed off at:

2) The cause:

3) What part of self is affected?
Self-Esteem, Pride, Ambition, Security,
Personal Relations, Pocket Book

4) What was my part?

5) Where are my mistakes?
Self-Seeking, Selfish, Dishonesty, Fear

6) Do I see any harm I caused?

7) Have I ever done the same thing?
YES   NO
(circle one)

8) Do I owe an amends?
YES   NO
(circle one)

Write about it.

Date:

1) I am pissed off at:

2) The cause:

3) What part of self is affected?
   Self-Esteem,   Pride,   Ambition,   Security,
      Personal Relations,   Pocket Book

4) What was my part?

5) Where are my mistakes?
   Self-Seeking,   Selfish,   Dishonesty,   Fear

6) Do I see any harm I caused?

7) Have I ever done the
   same thing?
   YES   NO
   (circle one)

8) Do I owe an amends?
   YES   NO
   (circle one)

Write about it.

Date:

1) I am pissed off at:

2) The cause:

3) What part of self is affected?
Self-Esteem, Pride, Ambition, Security, Personal Relations, Pocket Book

4) What was my part?

5) Where are my mistakes?
Self-Seeking, Selfish, Dishonesty, Fear

6) Do I see any harm I caused?

7) Have I ever done the same thing?
YES NO
(circle one)

8) Do I owe an amends?
YES NO
(circle one)

Write about it.

Date:

1) I am pissed off at:

2) The cause:

3) What part of self is affected?
Self-Esteem, Pride, Ambition, Security, Personal Relations, Pocket Book

4) What was my part?

5) Where are my mistakes?
Self-Seeking, Selfish, Dishonesty, Fear

6) Do I see any harm I caused?

7) Have I ever done the same thing?
YES   NO
(circle one)

8) Do I owe an amends?
YES   NO
(circle one)

Write about it.

Date:

1) I am pissed off at:

2) The cause:

3) What part of self is affected?
Self-Esteem, Pride, Ambition, Security,
Personal Relations, Pocket Book

4) What was my part?

5) Where are my mistakes?
Self-Seeking, Selfish, Dishonesty, Fear

6) Do I see any harm I caused?

7) Have I ever done the same thing?
YES   NO
(circle one)

8) Do I owe an amends?
YES   NO
(circle one)

Write about it.

Date:

1) I am pissed off at:

2) The cause:

3) What part of self is affected?
Self-Esteem, Pride, Ambition, Security,
Personal Relations, Pocket Book

4) What was my part?

5) Where are my mistakes?
Self-Seeking, Selfish, Dishonesty, Fear

6) Do I see any harm I caused?

7) Have I ever done the same thing?
YES   NO
(circle one)

8) Do I owe an amends?
YES   NO
(circle one)

Write about it.

Date:

1) I am pissed off at:

2) The cause:

3) What part of self is affected?
   Self-Esteem, Pride, Ambition, Security, Personal Relations, Pocket Book

4) What was my part?

5) Where are my mistakes?
   Self-Seeking, Selfish, Dishonesty, Fear

6) Do I see any harm I caused?

7) Have I ever done the same thing?
   YES   NO
   (circle one)

8) Do I owe an amends?
   YES   NO
   (circle one)

Write about it.

Date:

1) I am pissed off at:

2) The cause:

3) What part of self is affected?
   Self-Esteem,   Pride,   Ambition,   Security,
       Personal Relations,   Pocket Book

4) What was my part?

5) Where are my mistakes?
   Self-Seeking,   Selfish,   Dishonesty,   Fear

6) Do I see any harm I caused?

7) Have I ever done the
   same thing?
   YES   NO
   (circle one)

8) Do I owe an amends?
   YES   NO
   (circle one)

Write about it.

Date:

1) I am pissed off at:

2) The cause:

3) What part of self is affected?
   Self-Esteem,   Pride,   Ambition,   Security,
        Personal Relations,   Pocket Book

4) What was my part?

5) Where are my mistakes?
   Self-Seeking,   Selfish,   Dishonesty,   Fear

6) Do I see any harm I caused?

7) Have I ever done the same thing?
   YES   NO
   (circle one)

8) Do I owe an amends?
   YES   NO
   (circle one)

Write about it.

Date:

1) I am pissed off at:

2) The cause:

3) What part of self is affected?
Self-Esteem, Pride, Ambition, Security,
Personal Relations, Pocket Book

4) What was my part?

5) Where are my mistakes?
Self-Seeking, Selfish, Dishonesty, Fear

6) Do I see any harm I caused?

7) Have I ever done the
same thing?
YES   NO
(circle one)

8) Do I owe an amends?
YES   NO
(circle one)

Write about it.

Date:

1) I am pissed off at:

2) The cause:

3) What part of self is affected?
   Self-Esteem,   Pride,   Ambition,   Security,
        Personal Relations,   Pocket Book

4) What was my part?

5) Where are my mistakes?
   Self-Seeking,   Selfish,   Dishonesty,   Fear

6) Do I see any harm I caused?

7) Have I ever done the
   same thing?
   YES   NO
   (circle one)

8) Do I owe an amends?
   YES   NO
   (circle one)

Write about it.

Glossary

ANGRY
Why am I pissed off?
"Unreasonable fear that our instincts will not be satisfied drives us to covet the possessions of others, to lust for sex and power, to become <u>angry</u> when our instinctive demands are threatened, to be envious when the ambitions of others seem to be realized while ours are not." 12&12 p.49
"God save me from being angry." BB p.67

AMBITION
Ambition is what I want out of the scene.
"As to our grandiose behavior, we insisted that we had been possessed of nothing but a high and legitimate <u>ambition</u> to win the battle of life." 12&12 p.123

DISHONESTY
Dishonesty is the act or practice of telling a lie, omitting, cheating, deceiving, stealing etc.
"Continue to watch for selfishness, <u>dishonesty</u>, resentment, and fear." BB pg.84

ENVY
Envy has to do with things-wanting someone else's possessions
"The greatest enemies of us alcoholics (or addicts) are resentment, jealousy, <u>envy</u>, frustration and fear." BB p.145

FALSE PRIDE
False pride is either feeling better than, or less than
someone else. Feelings of superiority include prejudice
about race, education, or religious beliefs; sarcasm-
putting someone else down to make us feel better about
ourselves. Feelings of inferiority include self-pity-dwelling
on one's own problems, and low self-esteem-the lack of
self-worth, or respect.
*"So false pride became the reverse side of that ruinous coin
marked "Fear." 12&12 p.123*

FEAR
Fear is a feeling of anxiety, agitation, uneasiness,
apprehension
"We ask Him to remove our fear and direct our attention to
what He would have us be." BB p.68

INTIMATE (and SEX) RELATIONS
Intimate (and Sex) Relations is my deep-seeded ideas of
how a man/or woman would be in this situation.
*"No outsider can appraise such an intimate situation.
BBp.82*
*"We subjected each relation to this test–was it selfish, or
not?" BB p.69*

JEALOUSY
Jealousy has to do with people-being suspicious of
another's motives or doubting the faithfulness of a friend.
*"Keep it always in sight that we are dealing with the most
terrible human emotion–jealousy." BB p.82*

LAZINESS

Laziness means lacking the will or the desire to work. Procrastination, which is postponing or delaying an assigned job or task, is a form of laziness.

"And with the genuine alarm at the prospect of work, we stay lazy." 12&12 p.49

PERSONAL RELATIONS

Personal Relations is my deep-seeded idea of what this type of relationship is supposed to look like.

"Calm, thoughtful reflection upon personal relations can deepen our insight." 12&12 p.80

POCKET BOOK

Relates to my finances

"In most cases it was found that our self-esteem, our pocketbooks, our ambitions, our personal relations (including sex) were hurt or threatened."

PRIDE

Pride is how the rest of the actors are supposed to see me. "The world is but a stage."

"For pride, leading to self-justification, and always spurred by conscious or unconscious fears is the basic breeder of most human difficulties, the chief block to true progress." 12&12 p.48

"If you think you are an atheist, an agnostic, a skeptic, or have any other form of intellectual pride which keeps you from accepting what is in this book, I feel sorry for you." Dr. Bob speaking on the Big Book

SECURITY

Security is what I need out of this scene to be ok.

"We were still trying to find emotional security by being dominating, or dependent upon others." 12&12 p.116

"After we come into AA, if we go on growing, our attitudes and actions toward security, emotional security, and financial security—commence to change profoundly. 12&12 p.115

SELFISH

Selfish is too much concern with one's own welfare or interests and having little or no concern for others.

"Best of all, I met a kind doctor who explained that though certainly selfish and foolish, I had been seriously ill, bodily and mentally." BB p.7

SELF-ESTEEM

Self-esteem is my stage personality. The role I have assigned myself.

"...self esteem (fear); security." BB p.65

SELF-SEEKING

Self-seeking: is when a person seeks only, or mainly to further his own interests. This is important. Look at the resentment in its entirety, what is your part? Where are you to blame.

"Self-seeking will slip away." BB p.84

Made in the USA
Coppell, TX
22 April 2022

76916657R00069